The
CREATIVE
POWER
of SOUND

The CREATIVE POWER of SOUND

Affirmations to Create, Heal and Transform

ELIZABETH CLARE PROPHET

SUMMIT UNIVERSITY 🕊 PRESS®

THE CREATIVE POWER OF SOUND
Affirmations to Create, Heal and Transform
by Elizabeth Clare Prophet.

Copyright © 1998 by Summit University Press.
All rights reserved.

ISBN 0-922729-42-5

SUMMIT UNIVERSITY ☙ PRESS®
Summit University Press and ☙ are registered trademarks.
Printed in the United States of America.

03 02 01 00 99 98   6 5 4 3 2 1

CONTENTS

CONTENTS

WHEN I TAPPED INTO
A HIGHER POWER

*W*hen I was a teenager, I learned to tap into a universal power, a power available to all of us. In 1957, as a freshman at Antioch College in Yellow Springs, Ohio, I had one of several startling experiences with this power.

It was spring break, and at the last minute I realized that I didn't want to spend it in the dorm. I wanted to go home, back to Red Bank, New Jersey. But I had no ride and no money for the trip.

I went for a walk and called out loud to God, "God, I have to get home and you've gotta get me there!" I returned to my dorm and ran up the three flights of stairs to my room. The answer to my call came so fast, it almost took my breath away. For as I reached the top of the open stairwell, a voice yelled out, "Does anybody need a ride to New Jersey?"

"I do!" I said.

The voice belonged to an air force man from Wright-Patterson Air Force Base. Should I accept a ride from a stranger? My dorm sisters were worried, but I knew I would be safe with him because he was the answer to my call.

I packed my things and piled into the car. Exhausted from four days of finals, I went to sleep in the backseat. I slept for most of the trip, and my God-sent driver delivered me safely to my doorstep.

I knew I was onto something. I had tapped into a power of the universe by speaking my request. When I made a direct request *aloud,* God answered.

Several years before, I had read about a method of prayer called decrees in books by Guy and Edna Ballard of the "I AM" Religious Activity. Decrees are positive affirmations that use the name of God, I AM THAT I AM. By using these affirmations, you can access the power of your Higher Self.

In 1961, I attended a meeting of The Summit Lighthouse, where I met its founder, Mark Prophet, who would become both my teacher and my husband. Mark was able to receive inspired revelations from spiritual beings known as Ascended Masters. (The Ascended Masters are the saints and sages of East and West, such as Jesus, Buddha, Kuan Yin, Saint Francis and the Blessed Mother.) The Masters gave Mark many decrees, which he then published. When I, too, began receiving revelations from the Ascended Masters, I wrote down additional decrees.

Decrees are part of a system of prayer called the science of the spoken Word, which also includes songs, mantras and chants as well as visualizations and breathing techniques. I have published many books and lessons that teach people how to use the science of the spoken Word, and I've received innumerable letters from people who have used it successfully.

The primary purpose of using the science of the spoken Word, as you will see, is not to make good things happen—like getting a ride home or a new car—but to put you in contact with your Higher Self and with the Ascended Masters. Of course, once you have that contact, you can draw on the power of the God within to bring you the things you need in your life.

I invite you to experiment with the techniques in this pamphlet—and see how, when and where the universe will respond instantly to *your* call.

Elizabeth Clare Prophet

NOTE: All the stories in this book are real. Some names, however, have been changed at the individuals' request.

POWERFUL
AFFIRMATIONS
CALLED DECREES

*S*usan, a social worker, used these affirmations to overcome alcoholism, anxiety and depression. Jay, a computer programmer, used them to help him deal calmly with workplace jibes and has discovered added benefits. Andrew, a surgeon, thinks they help his patients. All three use them to get in touch with their Higher Self.

These powerful affirmations are called decrees. You are about to learn the science of the spoken Word, a method of using decrees to access the power of God inside of you. It relies on ancient principles as well as modern revelations given to Mark Prophet and me. For thirty years, people all over the world have been using the science of the spoken Word with surprising, even life-changing results.

Louise experiments with decrees

Take Louise, for example. She was a premed student when a friend gave her our book *The Science of the Spoken Word* (see p. 103). She began reading the book while living in a mountain cabin. She snuggled into her heated water bed, the only source of warmth, and read up to page 51, where she found specific instructions for decreeing.

"Sit in a comfortable straight chair," she read. "Hold your spine and head erect, your legs and hands uncrossed, and your feet flat on the floor." "Right," she told herself, laughing. It sounded pat, like a Weight Watchers commercial: Do this and you'll find God.

She wasn't about to get out of her warm bed and put her feet on the icy floor. So she said to herself, "OK, I'll try it. I'll do at least one thing that it told me to do. I'll say the words."

Louise began repeating aloud the decree "Adoration to God" (p. 92) and felt an immediate burning sensation in her heart. She was astonished. In the past, she had experienced this sensation only under certain circumstances—when she was in a meditative state either horseback riding or contemplating nature. This sensation had always been her indicator that she was close to God and it had usually taken her hours to find that closeness. Now she experienced it without preparation, while lying in bed.

The burning in her heart convinced

Louise that decrees worked and that they were a means of getting in touch with her Higher Self and finding inner peace. Now she uses decrees to find a feeling of closeness to God wherever she is, even while stuck in a traffic jam: "I wouldn't be able to find that peace here in the city now if I hadn't learned how to decree."

Since her first experience in the mountain cabin, Louise has used decrees regularly. She says they have helped in every area of her life—from resolving pain connected with her mother's alcoholism to finishing college, going on to law school and starting a professional career.

SEVEN FUNDAMENTAL
PRINCIPLES
OF THE SCIENCE OF THE SPOKEN WORD

$\mathcal{L}$ouise began her experiment with decrees by learning the seven fundamental principles of the science of the spoken Word. Once you've learned them, you'll be on the road to finding the benefits discovered by Louise and thousands of others who regularly use the science of the spoken Word to tap into the power of the Higher Self.

These are the seven principles:

1. *You can use prayer to create spiritual and material changes in your life.*
2. *Spoken prayer is more effective than silent prayer.*

3. *Decrees are* the *most powerful and effective form of spoken prayer.*
4. *When you use God's name, I AM THAT I AM, in your decrees, you access his unlimited power.*
5. *Repeating decrees increases their benefit.*
6. *Using visualizations enhances your decrees.*
7. *You can use breathing techniques to increase the power of your prayers and decrees.*

After you read the following seven sections, which explain these principles, you will be ready for the eighth section, "How to Decree." If you'd like to experiment with the spoken Word along the way, you can give the fiats—short, powerful decrees—in each section.

❧ 1 ❧

You Can Use Prayer to Create Spiritual and Material Changes in Your Life

Scientists don't know why or how it works. But an increasing number of studies suggest what people have known intuitively for thousands of years: prayer does work. It almost doesn't matter to whom you pray; the simple act of expressing desire to a higher power brings results.

One well-known study found that coronary patients at San Francisco General Hospital who were prayed for did better than those who were not prayed for. The patients who received prayers required fewer antibiotics and were less likely to develop certain complications than those who didn't receive prayers. One doctor said of the coronary study, "Maybe we doctors ought to be writing on our order sheets, 'Pray three times a day.' If it works, it works."[1]

Another study, at Dartmouth-Hitchcock Medical Center, examined how patients' own prayers affected their recovery from open-heart surgery. This 1995 study found that patients who said they drew comfort and strength from religious faith, which presumably included prayer, were three times more likely to survive in the six months following surgery than "nonreligious" patients.

Some people are skeptical of studies like these, believing that people's expectations of getting well influence the results. Consequently, many studies have been done on animals and plants. These studies, which all used control groups that were not prayed for, have found that mice, seeds and even mold and red blood cells could be healed or protected by prayer. (See *Healing Words* by Larry Dossey.)

The studies show how powerful the mind can be and suggest that prayer works. They demonstrate a principle you may have already discovered for yourself—you can use prayer to create spiritual and material changes in your life. The affirmations known as decrees are a powerful form of prayer. Once you become proficient at using them, you'll be able to use this principle even more effectively.

FIAT

LET THE LIGHT EXPAND
IN THE CENTER OF MY HEART!

SOME DOCTORS USE MORE THAN MEDICINE TO TREAT THEIR PATIENTS

Eighty-two percent of Americans believe in the healing power of personal prayer, and 64 percent think doctors should pray with their patients if the patients request it.[2] But many doctors are uncomfortable with this role. However, it may be time for a reassessment if the experiences of Andrew, a surgeon, and Nancy, an anesthesiologist, are any indication.

Andrew regularly decrees up to two hours a day, including prayers for his patients. Before surgery he gives a simple prayer, sometimes silently and other times (with the patient's consent) out loud. He credits his prayers and decrees with everything from contributing to the success of operations to helping relieve severe pain.

Once Andrew saw a patient's severe kidney pain alleviated in response to his prayer.

It was an acute situation and the woman was not yet on any pain medication. Andrew made a quick prayer to Jesus, Mother Mary and the healing angels to take away her pain. Without any medication, the pain vanished. "It was really dramatic," he says. "As soon as I said the prayer, she said her pain was gone." Results like this have convinced him to keep his patients in his decrees and prayers.

Nancy, an anesthesiologist, also found that decrees and prayers to the angels and the Ascended Masters made a difference. She kept up a regular routine of decrees at home; during work, she would say quick prayers.

When she decreed for women who were having difficulty giving birth, they were usually spared medical intervention. After being called to go to the delivery room to give anesthesia in preparation for a C-section, Nancy would give fiats and prayers in the stairwell on the way down. "It was amazing to me that often by the time I got there, the labor had suddenly progressed and I had arrived in time to see a baby being born," she recalls. "The nurses would grin, look at me and say, 'Guess we don't need you after all.'"

Nancy frequently prays to Kuan Yin, whom Buddhists call the Bodhisattva of Compassion. She believes that Kuan Yin helped to save the life of a woman who almost died during what should have been a routine operation to remove an ovarian cyst.

When the surgeon cut into the apparent cyst, it began

bleeding profusely. It turned out not to be a cyst at all but a swollen artery that had been accidentally tied off in a former surgery. The woman quickly began bleeding to death. The doctors tried all of the standard emergency procedures, including infusing massive amounts of fluid and blood. But after four hours, her heart stopped beating and her blood pressure was gone.

At that point, Nancy made a silent prayer, "Kuan Yin, help!" The next second, the patient's heart started beating again and her blood pressure returned. She recovered fully, without brain damage.

Although the experiences of Andrew and Nancy do not *prove* that decrees work, they suggest that both doctors and patients might want to experiment further with the power of the spoken Word.

*In the beginning was Brahman
with whom was the Word,
and the Word is Brahman.*

HINDU SCRIPTURES

*In the beginning was the Word,
and the Word was with God,
and the Word was God.*

THE GOSPEL OF JOHN

❧ 2 ❧

Spoken Prayer Is More Effective than Silent Prayer

Genesis tells us that God began the process of creation by speaking. He *said,* "Let there be light," and the universe began.

Is sound so powerful? Well, sound does more than ripple through our eardrums. We know it can be a dramatic destructive force —the high-pitched note that shatters a wineglass, the sonic boom that cracks plaster, the gunshot that sets off an avalanche.

But sound is also a constructive force, as doctors and health practitioners are discovering every day. Ultrasound (high-pitched sound waves) is being used for everything from cleaning wounds to diagnosing tumors to pulverizing kidney stones. Someday it may even be used to inject drugs into the body, making needles obsolete.

Scientists are now researching sound's impact on the brain. Certain kinds of classical music, like Bach, Mozart and Beethoven, have a range of positive effects, including temporarily raising IQ, expanding memory and speeding learning. Some alternative medical practitioners are experimenting with using specific tones to heal the organs. Other researchers are looking at the effects of some of the sounds that originate in the human voice box—prayer and chanting.

Sound, the energy of creation

Some people chant for relaxation or healing; others to contact God and the infinite. But many people are also discovering that sound is the energy that causes things to come into being, to exist. It's the energy that can create. And if we use the energy of sound properly, we can create positive change in every area of life.

For centuries, mystics have been telling us that sound actually creates matter. (A mystic is someone who seeks direct contact or union with God.) The mystics believe the world is a reflection of infinite combinations of sound patterns. They say that all things—from the biggest star to the smallest flower and even you and I—are coagulations of sound waves.

This may be difficult to understand, let

alone believe. But science has provided some corroboration for the mystics' assertion. On a cosmic scale, there may be evidence that sound has left its imprint on the galaxies. Some scientists argue that the galaxies are not arranged at random but in a regular pattern of clusters. Now researchers are suggesting that it was primordial sound waves that helped create this pattern of clusters.[3]

On a smaller scale, Hans Jenny, a Swiss scientist, passed sound waves through various kinds of malleable matter, such as paste and sand. (See photographs, p. 27.) When we look at the patterns created by these waves, we can begin to imagine how creation by sound might occur.

*And the song of all six heavens
was not only heard but seen.*

THE VISION OF ISAIAH,
second-century Jewish-Christian text

In the 1960s, Swiss scientist Hans Jenny demonstrated the creative power of sound in a series of experiments in which he made sound vibrations visible. He sent vibrations at different frequencies into a variety of substances, such as sand, paste and metal filings. These vibrations created patterns that mimicked natural structures—from the very big, like galaxies, to the very small, like human cells. A crescendo of sound caused powder evenly sprinkled on a plate to form a pattern resembling the human iris (upper right). A different frequency caused the powder to shape itself into the flowing form of the T'ai Chi (middle right). And vibrating sand mirrored a spiral galaxy (bottom right).

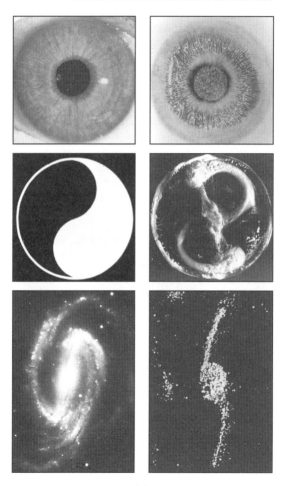

How mantras and chants harness sound

The sound by which all things are created isn't just any sound. It's the Word of God. Hindu, Buddhist and Jewish mystics believe that this Word creates and pervades everything that exists. If we believe the mystics, the Word is the most powerful creative force in the universe.

And there is a way we can harness that force. The mystics of East and West have connected with the power of creation by repeating spoken mantras and the names of God.*

Hindu and Buddhist mystics believe mantras can unleash forces that can create or

---

*A mantra is a word or combination of words held to be sacred. Many mantras are composed of Sanskrit words. According to Hindu tradition, mantras were received by God-inspired sages who were able to listen to the fundamental tones of the universe.

destroy. Hindu writings tell us that yogis have used mantras, along with visualizations, to light fires, materialize physical objects (like food), bring rain and even influence the outcome of battles.

But producing physical changes wasn't their primary goal. They believed that mantras helped them to achieve enlightenment and oneness with God by bringing them protection and wisdom, enhancing their concentration and meditation, and simply propelling them back to God.

Hindus and Buddhists aren't the only ones who have used the power of the Word. Prayers are spoken, sung and chanted in churches, temples and mosques around the world. Christians pray the Our Father aloud in church. Jews give the Shema in their synagogues. Some Christian monks chant their prayers. Perhaps the practice is so widespread because people of many religions instinctively recognize the effectiveness of spoken prayer.

Shrī-Yantra: A yantra is a geometrical diagram used in meditation. The Shrī-Yantra (top) has been used for centuries in the East to represent the visual equivalent of a mantra. Sound waves passed through an electronic transmitter have mirrored the pattern of the yantra (bottom). Has science rediscovered what the ancients knew—that sound creates matter?

THE ENERGIZING POWER OF GREGORIAN CHANTS

One group of Benedictine monks discovered an unexpected benefit from their Gregorian chants: their chanting seemed to energize their bodies.

In 1967 Alfred Tomatis, a French physician, psychologist and ear specialist, studied how chanting affected the Benedictine monks. For hundreds of years they had kept a rigorous schedule, sleeping only a few hours a night and chanting from six to eight hours a day. When a new abbot changed the schedule and cut out the chanting, the monks became tired and lethargic. The more sleep they got, the more tired they seemed to become.

Tomatis was called in to find out what was wrong with them. He believed that chanting (and listening to certain kinds of music) served a special purpose—energizing the brain and body. He said the monks "had been chanting in order to 'charge' themselves."[4] He reintroduced chanting, along with a program of listening to stimulating sounds, and the monks soon found the energy to return to their normal schedule. Whether the monks knew it or not, they had discovered the power of sound, especially spoken or chanted prayer.

FIAT

LET GOD BE MAGNIFIED!

When Carla first heard about decrees, she couldn't understand why she had to give them out loud. "I was by nature inclined to silence and meditation," she says. "Decrees seemed like silly verses to me."

A persistent friend encouraged her to use decrees, so one day she decided to give them another try. She said a silent prayer, "God, explain to me why I should do this. If there's any value and positive action in decrees, show me!" As soon as she began to give the decree "I AM the Violet Flame" (p. 89), she had the following experience in which an angel answered her prayer:

I felt myself lifted into another realm of consciousness. An intense pink-white light enveloped me, and from behind I heard the rushing of powerful wings approaching at great speed. Somehow I knew that it was an angel.

Then I realized I was still giving the decree. I saw how the words of the decree were changed into energy that in turn formed into a large sphere of glowing white light right in front of my mouth. The moment the sphere formed, two beautiful hands plucked it from my lips and disappeared with it at lightning speed. Then the vision faded.

It all happened in a split second. The light around me subsided and I floated back into my normal consciousness. I don't know who the angel was, but I was left with a vivid understanding of what happens when we give decrees and I've given them ever since.

The LORD *is nigh unto all them that call upon him, to all that call upon him in truth.*

PSALM 145:18

FIAT

UNFAILING LIGHT OF GOD,
I AM CALLING YOUR PERFECTION
INTO ACTION IN ME NOW!

❧ 3 ❧

Decrees Are the Most Powerful and Effective Form of Spoken Prayer

---

No matter what religion you practice, you can add decrees to your devotions. Decreeing is the most effective and powerful way to harness God's energy. It's the key to changing yourself and the world.

Since spoken prayer is more effective than silent prayer, you should always give your decrees aloud. If you can't decree aloud —if you're in a public place, for instance— you can repeat the decrees in your mind. But you will soon discover through your own experience the incredible power you'll unleash when you practice the science of the *spoken* Word.

Lynette, an artist, proved this to herself

one night when she was awakened by an intruder in her bedroom. She could see him silhouetted in the doorway. How could she get him to leave? First she told him to go. "My neighbor will come if I scream," she said. "He won't have time," the intruder replied in a threatening tone.

Suddenly, she remembered Archangel Michael and began giving the "Traveling Protection" decree at the top of her lungs. Unlike her earlier attempt to get the intruder to leave, the decree had an immediate effect. The intruder turned and ran, yelling, "OK, I'll leave you alone, lady!" as he flew out the back door.

Here is the complete decree that she gave:

Lord Michael before!
Lord Michael behind!
Lord Michael to the right!
Lord Michael to the left!
Lord Michael above!
Lord Michael below!
Lord Michael, Lord Michael wherever I go!

I AM his love protecting here!
I AM his love protecting here!
I AM his love protecting here!

*Decrees can help you connect
with the energy of your Higher Self
to make the changes you want
in your life*

One reason decrees are so powerful is that
they form a direct link to your Higher Self,
who holds the keys of creation. Here's how:

Once, long before you were born on
earth, your soul was united with your
Higher Self. Lifetimes ago, you chose to live
apart from God, thus separating from your
Higher Self. But within your heart there still
burns a divine spark, your potential to be
one with God. And a stream of spiritual
energy known as the crystal cord connects
your divine spark with your Higher Self,
nourishing and sustaining you.

The science of the spoken Word does
two things:

1. *It increases the current of God's spiritual energy flowing over your crystal cord. You can then use this energy for whatever you want—to draw to yourself the things that you need; to find the right job, home and circumstance in life; to heal yourself and your loved ones; or to fix problems in your town or city.*

2. *It brings you closer to your Higher Self.*

To meet your Higher Self, give some of the decrees and fiats in this book with love and devotion. Then wait for the powerful return current of light, life and love. As you draw nearer to this Presence of God, you will find that it will lead you to the answers, the people and the circumstances you need to fulfill your purpose in life. Contacting your Higher Self could be the best thing that ever happened to you!

The partitions around Jay's work area couldn't keep out the noise—or the rude comments. As soon as he would begin to type at his computer, his coworkers would start in with belittling remarks and distracting noises. When he began suffering from diabetes, they even joked about his weight loss.

Jay felt he needed to do something to protect himself from these seemingly harmless remarks, which came laced with a wallop of negative energy. Since he had been practicing kung fu and chi kung (a Chinese system of energy control) for ten years, he had become sensitive to energy currents. He felt he was becoming a magnet for his coworkers' negative energy. He knew he needed to find a source of spiritual protection.

One of Jay's friends introduced him to the science of the spoken Word, and he began to give decrees for protection. The first two times he decreed, he felt goose bumps. He described them as going "all the way around me from my head down to my feet." Then he heard an inner voice say, "Finally he's asking us to help him." Jay knew he had found what he was looking for.

He began decreeing every day, adding decrees to his routine of kung fu and chi kung. When he experimented with decrees for love, transmutation and protection, he noticed an immediate benefit. Jay says his decrees have helped "counteract negative energy" and "bring down the light" from his Higher Self. The decrees have also helped him to "reprogram" himself so that he no longer responds to the negativity of his fellow workers. And through decrees, he finds that he can have his own space, even while surrounded by sarcasm and criticism.

Jay also believes that decrees help him to keep focused on God and have led to spiritual experiences and contact with his Higher Self and the Ascended Masters. He says the Masters have inspired him with visualizations and spiritual exercises that he uses along with his decrees to further neutralize the negativity of his surroundings. He believes the decrees opened the way for another unexpected benefit—his boss gave him a private office. Now he can decree during his breaks and work in peace.

FIAT

ARCHANGEL MICHAEL,
HELP ME! HELP ME! HELP ME!

‹ 4 ›

When You Use God's Name, I AM THAT I AM, in Your Decrees, You Access His Unlimited Power

When God spoke to Moses out of the burning bush, he revealed both his name, I AM THAT I AM, and the true nature of man. Exodus tells us that the bush "burned with fire, and the bush was not consumed."[5] The bush symbolizes you and the fire symbolizes your divine spark. This spark is a spiritual flame of God's fire that burns within you yet does not consume you, just as the bush was not consumed.

The true nature of man that God revealed to Moses is what is known as the I AM Presence. It's called the "I AM" Presence in reference to God's name, I AM

THAT I AM. The I AM Presence is the individualized Presence of God that he gave you when he created you. (In a broad sense, you can think of your I AM Presence together with your Holy Christ Self[6] as your Higher Self.)

At the burning bush, God instructed Moses to tell the children of Israel that his name is I AM THAT I AM and that "this is my name for ever, and this is my memorial unto all generations." The Jerusalem Bible translates this sentence as: "This is my name for all time; *by this name I shall be invoked* for all generations to come."[7] You see, God himself gave us the authority to use his name to invoke him.

Jesus used God's name when he made the "I am" statements in the Gospel of John, such as "I am the resurrection and the life."[8]

We can take any of these affirmations and make them our own. When you say, "I AM THAT I AM," you're simply saying, "I, myself, am right here the I AM Presence of God that is above me." Every time you say, "I AM...," you are really saying, "God in me is...," and thus drawing to yourself whatever follows. For example, when you say, "I AM illumination," you are saying that God in you is attracting to you more illumination.*

"I AM" is more than a sacred name. It

*The principle of using "I AM THAT I AM" in prayer was developed by Emma Curtis Hopkins. She was first a student of Mary Baker Eddy, founder of Christian Science. Later Hopkins began teaching on her own and founded the popular religious movement called New Thought. In 1887, she began using the term "decree" to define positive affirmations preceded by "I AM," such as "I AM whole." In the early 1930s, Guy and Edna Ballard founded the "I AM" Religious Activity, which also used decrees. Since 1958, Mark and Elizabeth Prophet have received many new decrees from the Ascended Masters.

is an empowerment. It is a formula that unlocks God's authority and his energy of creation when it is given with love. When you use it, you are not setting yourself up as a god separate from God. Rather, you are affirming your oneness with God. You are saying, "God in me is giving this decree. God's energy is flowing through me, obeying the command I have given in his name. And God is fulfilling his law by the power of the spoken Word."

Now you know why many decrees and fiats use God's name, I AM THAT I AM.

FIAT

I AM THE RESURRECTION
AND THE LIFE!

❧ 5 ❧

*Repeating Decrees Increases
Their Benefit*

Decrees, fiats and mantras are all meant to be repeated. In the East, people repeat their mantras over and over, even thousands of times a day. But in the West we are not accustomed to the idea of repeating a prayer.

People often ask, "Why should I have to ask God for something more than once?" The answer is that repeating a prayer is not simply making a request over and over. Each time you repeat a prayer, you strengthen the power of the request by qualifying it with more and more of God's light-energy. You also begin to enter into a state of oneness with God.

The benefits of repetitive prayer have

been demonstrated by both mystics and scientists. The mystics of the Eastern Orthodox Church have a tradition of repeating the simple prayer "Lord Jesus Christ, Son of God, have mercy upon me" thousands of times a day. Over the centuries, monks who have done this have reported extraordinary mystical experiences and a feeling of oneness with God.

Medieval monks claimed that after several weeks of repeating the prayer for many hours a day, they entered an altered state. They said they could see a powerful light around them, which they compared to the light the disciples saw on Jesus' face and garments when he was transfigured. One mystic described the condition as a "most pleasant heat," a "joyful boiling." He claimed to exist in a state beyond pleasure and pain, experiencing a "lightness and freshness, pleasantness of living, insensibility to sickness and sorrows."[9] This is a state in which the flesh is "kindled by the Spirit, so that the whole man becomes spiritual."[10]

Many mystics East and West who repeat prayers or chant mantras have reported similar experiences, as have people who decree. But for centuries, skeptics pooh-poohed repetitive prayer as a superstition without measurable benefit—until a doctor at Harvard Medical School documented beneficial *physical* effects from repetitive prayer, including the very prayer the monks had been using for centuries.

*Saying your prayers over and over
may be good for your health*

In the early 1970s, Dr. Herbert Benson, president and founder of the Mind/Body Medical Institute at Harvard Medical School, documented a phenomenon he dubbed "the relaxation response," which he says is the opposite of the body's fight-or-flight mechanism.

Benson experimented using Sanskrit mantras. He told his subjects to sit quietly and repeat the prayer either mentally or verbally for ten to twenty minutes, to breathe regularly and to push intruding thoughts aside as they entered their minds.

Benson found that those who repeated the Sanskrit mantras, for as little as ten minutes a day, experienced physiological changes —reduced heart rate, lower stress levels and slower metabolism. Repeating the mantras also lowered the blood pressure of those who had high blood pressure and generally decreased the subjects' oxygen consumption (indicating that the body was in a restful state). Subsequent studies documented in Benson's *Timeless Healing* found that repeating mantras can benefit the immune system, relieve insomnia, reduce doctor visits and even increase high-school sophomores' self-esteem.

Benson and his colleagues also tested other prayers, including "Lord Jesus Christ, have mercy on me," and found that they had the same effect. Even words like *one, ocean, love* and *peace* produced the response. It appears that Benson and his colleagues had uncovered a universal principle: repetitive prayer allows human beings to enter a relaxed state.

Repeating prayers has spiritual benefits too

Benson documented the physical effects of repeating prayers, but what about the spiritual benefits? Hindus and Buddhists tell us that repetition allows the mind to focus on God. This makes it easier to become one with your Higher Self. Eastern Orthodox monks found joy, happiness and oneness with God through repetitive prayer. Jewish mystics described a similar feeling after repeating the names of God. They called it a transforming moment in which they entered the highest state of consciousness possible for human beings. This goal—entering a higher state of consciousness, a state of oneness with God—is why people repeat their decrees, chants, mantras and prayers.

Many who have decreed have felt this

oneness with God. Ann, who has decreed for fifteen years, says that repeating her decrees makes her feel one with God: "You get to a point where you feel that your I AM Presence is decreeing through you, that you're the vessel and that the I AM Presence is doing the work. You are connected to God; but it's not your power, it's God's. You're in sync with God. It's a high that's different from any artificial high that you could get."

You'll find decrees in the back of this book that will allow you not only to find the state known as the relaxation response but also to probe the heights of your higher reality.

Repeating your decrees allows you to "stock up" on spiritual energy

Another benefit of repeating your decrees is that you build a momentum of positive energy that you can use in moments of great need. You can think of it as stocking a reservoir. When you build this momentum or reservoir, it's there in an emergency, such as a car accident or a dangerous situation. You can then draw upon it by giving a powerful fiat.

Davies, a retired electronics engineer, began decreeing when he belonged to the "I AM" Religious Activity in the 1930s. He used this principle while returning from a spiritual conference in Los Angeles, where he had given many hours of decrees. He was sixteen years old and was riding in a car with his mother, brother and two friends. His mother started pulling the car over onto the shoulder of the road, but the shoulder was soft and couldn't support the car. She lost control and the car flew into the air.

Immediately, Davies said the name of Jesus, which he had learned to give as a powerful fiat to invoke protection: "Jesus Christ!" While some people might have said those words with a different meaning, he used them as a passkey to access his reservoir of light. The next thing he knew, the car had come to a halt upright. No one was seriously injured, although the car was totaled.

Davies believes that the response to his fiat was so powerful and immediate because he tapped into the reservoir of light he had stocked during the conference. At age seventy-three, he still decrees.

I am the light of the world.

JESUS, as recorded in John 8:12

FIAT

I AM THE LIGHT WHICH LIGHTETH
EVERY MAN THAT COMETH INTO
THE WORLD.

❧ 6 ❧

*Using Visualizations Enhances
Your Decrees*

Mantra means "instrument of the mind." What you think about when you are decreeing or giving mantras makes a big difference in how powerful and effective your decrees are. Someone who is focusing on their decrees can accomplish more in five minutes than someone else who decrees all day without concentrating.

Your attitude and thoughts while you decree are crucial. When you decree, you should visualize, or see, a mental image. As you become more familiar with the decrees, you can close your eyes as you repeat them and strengthen your concentration on the mental image.

Your primary focus while decreeing should always be your I AM Presence, which you can see as a blazing sun of light overhead. You can also concentrate on the divine spark in your heart, imagining it as a dazzling sphere of light as brilliant as the sun at noonday. As you decree, see thousands of sunbeams going forth from your heart as light rays to heal and comfort every child of God on earth.

You can also look at any of the following pictures—your favorite saint or Ascended Master, a natural or man-made symmetrical pattern that represents the perfection of God (like a star, galaxy, flower, plant or geometric form), a beautiful scene from nature or a great work of art.

Sometimes the decree itself evokes a mental image. The "Salutation to the Sun"

(p. 83) describes welcoming the light into your life, mind, spirit and soul. You can visualize the light descending from your I AM Presence and coalescing around your body, dissolving your problems and precipitating the circumstances that you need.

When you give the "Traveling Protection" decree (p. 39), you're invoking Archangel Michael. As you say, "Lord Michael before! Lord Michael behind...," visualize great blue angels all around you. This is a great decree to give while driving. You can visualize Archangel Michael and his angels surrounding every car on the road. As you say, "I AM his love protecting here," you can see Archangel Michael protecting everyone on earth.

During decrees you can also concentrate on something you desire, making sure always to ask for your request to be adjusted according to your soul's needs. If your attention is riveted on what you want and your mind's eye is visualizing it as well, the results will be infinitely more effective than if your mind wanders, you are distracted and your eyes gaze at random around the room. If you do become distracted, don't condemn yourself. Instead, gently return your mind to your focus.

You may find that adding visualizations to your decrees may help you bridge the gap between the spiritual and the material worlds and truly produce magic in your life.

FIAT

LET THE LIGHT EXPAND
IN THE CENTER OF MY HEART!

❦ 7 ❧

*You Can Use Breathing Techniques
to Increase the Power of Your
Prayers and Decrees*

The breath and the mind are connected. By consciously controlling your breathing, you can calm and focus your mind and enter higher states of consciousness. The slow, rhythmic breathing that accompanies chanting and repetitive prayer may be partly responsible for its beneficial physical effects.

Before you start your decree session, take a slow, deep breath. Blow all of the air out of your lungs, then breathe in slowly. This allows the Spirit of God to enter your body. You may wish to say Om or I AM THAT I AM slowly and in one breath before you begin your session.

As you decree, keep your breathing slow and rhythmic. Never let yourself get out of breath. Try to slow down your breath so that you say as many words as possible in one breath. In this way, your lungs cooperate with your brain and vocal cords to draw down the maximum amount of light from your I AM Presence.

FIAT

IN THE NAME OF THE LIGHT OF GOD
THAT NEVER FAILS,
I AM THE MIRACLE OF GOD!
AND I ACCEPT A MIRACLE THIS DAY!

DECREES AND THE 12-STEPPER

It had been a rough road through drugs, alcohol and bulimia. Susan hit bottom in 1983 and joined Alcoholics Anonymous. "Without alcohol in me, I felt so totally alone," she says. "I felt like I was in a black hole in life and that I was just going to die. And I was glad, because I couldn't figure out how I was going to live." She was fearful and depressed. "I was so full of fear, I could hardly relate to people or talk to people," she says.

She began decreeing again. (She had started, then stopped, three years before.) She saw the decrees as an adjunct to the 12-step work she was doing in Alcoholics Anonymous. One of the goals of the program is putting your trust in a higher power.

She felt that the decrees were helping her accomplish that goal.

She began decreeing two to two-and-a-half hours every night to help overcome the fear that had swept in once she had removed the artificial high of alcoholism. "Nighttime was the worst time," she recalls. "I'd be scared to death of anything." But she soon found that the decrees "helped lift my consciousness out of the human realm."

"I would just stand there and decree and feel a part of the light," she says. "Little by little, the levels of fear that had been plaguing me were replaced with the love and security of the I AM Presence." By reconnecting her to the I AM Presence, the decrees helped her overcome the sense of separation from God that had led to her drinking in the first place.

She found that in her communion with

her I AM Presence, she was able to enter a state that she calls "total joy and love and understanding of others." This helped her get over feelings of hurt from past problems in relationships. And it helped her accept one of the principles of the 12-step program: Don't rely on other people, because they will always let you down. Instead, rely on your higher power. "People are not going to give me what I want," Susan says. "What I want I can get from the Ascended Masters and my I AM Presence. My satisfaction comes from God."

Today Susan, in her forties, is happily married with two small girls and a fulfilling career as a social worker. She believes she overcame her alcoholism by using the 12-step program and her decrees. She needed the systematic approach of the 12-step program, but she also needed the light she invoked in her decrees to get her through. The two systems "correlate perfectly with each other," she says. The decrees helped her to stick to the program and to find "true wholeness," a feeling of oneness with God that replaced the "false wholeness" she got from alcohol.

FIAT

I AND MY FATHER ARE ONE!
I AND MY MOTHER ARE ONE!

HOW TO DECREE

*N*ow you're ready to begin experimenting with the science of the spoken Word. But before you start, ask yourself what you want to get out of your decrees.

Do you have spiritual goals or practical goals? Spiritual goals might include being more loving, drawing closer to your Higher Self or overcoming painful childhood experiences that create problems in your relationships. Practical goals might include finding a new job, getting the money to finish your education or meeting new friends.

You may also have goals for other people, your nation or the planet. Perhaps you want to get gangs out of your neighborhood, keep drunk drivers off the road, help someone with chronic pain or illness, or stop bloodshed in the Middle East.

Before you begin decreeing, make a list of your goals, which you'll want to update periodically.

Spiritual Goals: _____

_____

_____

_____

_____

_____

Practical Goals: _____

_____

_____

_____

_____

_____

After you've listed your goals, you can get ready to decree. You can give decrees anywhere, even while you're doing chores, going for a walk or driving. But you should try to spend at least some time each day decreeing in a quiet place, with no interruptions, at an altar you've consecrated—a closet or a corner of your bedroom or living room. You can put on your altar candles, crystals, flowers and photographs of saints, Ascended Masters and those for whom you are praying. Have the room well-lit, clean and aired. (Poor lighting, dust, untidiness and stale air make your decrees less effective by impeding the flow of spiritual energy.)

It's important to have the correct posture when decreeing. You can decree standing, sitting in a chair or in the lotus position used by Hindus and Buddhists. If you sit, make sure your chair is comfortable and straight backed. Hold your spine and head erect. Keep your legs and hands uncrossed and your feet flat on the floor. Poor posture opens the consciousness to negative influences. Crossing your legs and hands short-circuits the energies that are intended to flow through you to bless all mankind.

Hold your written decree at eye level so you're not leaning down while decreeing. You can even sit at a desk or table so you can prop up your decree in front of you, leaving your hands free. When your hands are free, separate them, rest them in your lap and cup them, palms up. The index finger of each hand can touch the thumb.

Next, give a prayer or invocation naming where you want to direct the light-energy you invoke. Then choose a decree from the back of this book. Speak the decree with devotion, love and feeling. Begin slowly and at the pitch of your normal speaking voice. Endow each word with intense love for God, holding in mind your chosen visualization.

Speaking the decree slowly allows you to achieve a deep, heartfelt communion with God. As you repeat the decree, you can gradually increase both the speed and pitch. Although speeding up is not essential, the acceleration will increase the ability of your decrees to dissolve negative thoughts or energies that have attached themselves to you. You should consciously increase the speed of your decrees only if you feel the need; the decree should almost speed itself up.

Repeat the decree three or nine times to begin with. When you're ready, you can begin to increase your repetitions. Repeating a decree 36, 40, 108 or even 144 times can access more of the creative power of sound.

As you repeat a decree, you'll feel it take on a natural rhythm. The rhythm is one of the things that gives a decree its power. Just as the rhythm of an army marching in step can collapse a bridge, so the rhythm of decrees can create a strong spiritual force that breaks down accumulations of negative energy, habit patterns and karma. The rhythm also sets up a vibratory pattern that sends the light you have invoked across the planet.

To learn the proper rhythm, tone and speed with which to decree, you can practice decreeing with the audiotapes and CDs published by Church Universal and Triumphant. (For information, see p. 102.)

How to get what you need from God

When you decree, visualize yourself receiving the things you need. Always ask for your requests to God to be adjusted by your Higher Self according to whatever is best for your soul and the souls of those for whom you are decreeing.

When you use the science of the spoken Word, you are decreeing by God's authority, and God will answer you in the way that is best for your soul. Don't be disappointed if your requests are not immediately answered. Your Higher Self may be trying to lead you in another direction, one that ultimately will bring greater soul growth.

Be prepared for results, even if they are not the ones you are looking for. Remember, God said, "Prove me now herewith, if I will not open you the windows of heaven and pour you out a blessing, that there shall not be room enough to receive it!"[11]

Even if you are able to decree for just a few minutes a day, it can make a difference in your mental outlook, your physical condition and in your relationship with God. Try the science of the spoken Word—and see what the light can do for you and what you can do for a world in need.

*Because he hath set his love upon me,
therefore will I deliver him....
He shall call upon me,
and I will answer him.*

PSALM 91:14, 15

*Thou shalt make thy prayer
unto him, and he shall hear thee....
Thou shalt also decree a thing,
and it shall be established unto thee:
and the light shall shine
upon thy ways.*

JOB 22:27, 28

DYNAMIC DECREES

Give the following preamble as you begin each session of decrees:

In the name of my I AM Presence, I call to the seven archangels and their legions of light. I call to _____

(Insert the names of saints and Ascended Masters.)

to direct your light, energy and consciousness to bless all of life and to help me accomplish the following goals: _____

(Use your list from p. 70.)

I ask my I AM Presence to adjust my requests in accordance with what is best for my soul and the souls of those for whom I am praying.

TUBE OF LIGHT

Instructions:

You can use this little decree to bring you closer to your I AM Presence and to build a powerful energy of protection around you. You should give the "Tube of Light" decree at least three times at the beginning of every decree session.

Visualization:

See a tube of fiery, opaque, white spiritual energy nine feet in diameter descending around you from your I AM Presence. See the tube block all negative energy directed at you. Then see the violet flame filling the tube, liberating you from your daily burdens.

Beloved I AM Presence bright,
Round me seal your Tube of Light
From Ascended Master flame
Called forth now in God's own name.
Let it keep my temple free
From all discord sent to me.

I AM calling forth violet fire
To blaze and transmute all desire,
Keeping on in Freedom's name
Till I AM one with the violet flame.

SALUTATION TO THE SUN

Instructions:

The following powerful decree can help you become one with your I AM Presence. Repeat the decree slowly at first, then more quickly as you get to know the words. Eventually you will reach the state in which your mind has become one with the prayer and goes on repeating it, even when your lips have stopped and you are once more involved in daily cares. You'll find that as you give this each day, you will manifest outwardly the divinity that is within you.

Visualization:

See spiritual energy (light) descending from your I AM Presence into your body, heart, mind and soul. See it expanding from your heart to create a large spherical ovoid of light that extends three feet from your body in all directions.

O mighty Presence of God, I AM,
    in and behind the Sun:
I welcome thy Light,
    which floods all the earth,
    into my life, into my mind,
    into my spirit, into my soul.
Radiate and blaze forth thy Light!
Break the bonds of darkness and superstition!
Charge me with the great clearness
    of thy white fire radiance!
I AM thy child, and each day I shall become
    more of thy manifestation!

I AM LIGHT

Instructions:

This decree helps to dissolve negative energy that has become attached to you. That energy can come from criticism, depression or anger (your own or others') as well as from fatigue or excessive noise and environmental pollution.

Visualization:

See the light in your heart as a blazing sun that expands to consume all of your burdens. See your crystal cord expand as your I AM Presence floods you with spiritual energy. Then see the light flowing from you to help everyone you meet.

I AM Light, glowing Light,
Radiating Light, intensified Light.
God consumes my darkness,
Transmuting it into Light.

This day I AM a focus of the Central Sun.
Flowing through me is a crystal river,
A living fountain of Light
That can never be qualified
By human thought and feeling.
I AM an outpost of the Divine.
Such darkness as has used me is swallowed up
By the mighty river of Light which I AM.

I AM, I AM, I AM Light;
I live, I live, I live in Light.
I AM Light's fullest dimension;
I AM Light's purest intention.
I AM Light, Light, Light
Flooding the world everywhere I move,
Blessing, strengthening and conveying
The purpose of the kingdom of heaven.

I AM PRESENCE,
THOU ART MASTER

Instructions:

This decree is especially useful for protection. Give it nine times each morning. It can help shield you from negative and aggressive energy. As you give this decree, you may feel yourself becoming one with your I AM Presence.

Visualization:

See the light of your I AM Presence descending into your form and transforming it into the image of God. And watch the blue lightning flashing forth from your I AM Presence. This blue lightning is an intense form of spiritual energy that dissolves negative energy on contact.

I AM Presence, Thou art Master,
I AM Presence, clear the way!
Let thy Light and all thy Power
Take possession here this hour!
Charge with Victory's mastery,
Blaze blue lightning, blaze thy substance!
Into this thy form descend,
That Perfection and its Glory
Shall blaze forth and earth transcend!

I AM THE VIOLET FLAME

Instructions:

The violet flame is a special gift from God —a spiritual fire that can transform negative energy into positive energy. It can bring you feelings of happiness and freedom in God. And you can use it to send forgiveness to anyone who has ever hurt you. Give this decree three times, twelve times or in multiples of three, increasing the repetitions as you memorize it.

Visualization:

The violet flame ranges in color from pale lilac to magenta to deep amethyst. You can imagine it working just like a giant chalkboard eraser, wiping out your feelings of pain, despair, suffering and limitation.

I AM the violet flame
    In action in me now
I AM the violet flame
    To Light alone I bow
I AM the violet flame
    In mighty cosmic power
I AM the Light of God
    Shining every hour
I AM the violet flame
    Blazing like a sun
I AM God's sacred power
    Freeing every one

BLUE LIGHTNING IS THY LOVE!

Instructions:

Before you give this decree, you can give a prayer to Archangel Michael and his legions of angels to place their protective energy around you as you go through the day.

Visualization:

Blue is the energy of protection. Archangel Michael and his angels most often appear dressed in blue-flame armour and surrounded by an intense blue and white light that looks like lightning. You can visualize yourself clothed in this armour with light surrounding you as you give this decree. Hold this image throughout the day to protect yourself from both physical dangers and harmful energies.

Blue lightning is thy Love,
Flood forth to free all;
Blue lightning is thy Power,
In God I see all;
Blue lightning is thy Mind,
In pure Truth I find

Light will overcome,
Light will make us one.
Light from blue-fire sun,
Command us now all free!

Blue lightning is thy Law,
Blaze forth as holy awe;
Blue lightning is thy Name,
Our heart's altar do enflame;
Blue lightning maketh free,
In God I'll ever be.

Light will overcome
Light will make us one
Light from blue-fire sun
Command us now all free!

ADORATION TO GOD

Instructions:

You can use this decree to help you feel closer to your Higher Self. Giving it once or three times a day may help you feel at peace with God and your loved ones.

Visualization:

See yourself ascending toward your I AM Presence. Feel the bliss of God as you are surrounded by a suffusion of beautiful pink light. Watch the light penetrate every cell of your body. As you are transformed, particle by particle, feel your oneness with God and with all creation.

Beloved Mighty I AM Presence,
Thou life that beats my heart,
Come now and take dominion,
Make me of thy life a part.
Rule supreme and live forever
In the flame ablaze within;
Let me from thee never sever,
Our reunion now begin.

All the days proceed in order
From the current of thy power,
Flowing forward like a river,
Rising upward like a tower.
I AM faithful to thy love ray
Blazing forth light as a sun;
I AM grateful for thy right way
And thy precious word "Well done."

I AM, I AM, I AM adoring Thee!   (give 3 times)
O God, you are so magnificent!   (give 9 times)
I AM, I AM, I AM adoring Thee!   (give 3 times)

(continued)

93

Moving onward to perfection,
I AM raised by Love's great grace
To thy center of direction—
Behold, at last I see thy face.
Image of immortal power,
Wisdom, love, and honor, too,
Flood my being now with glory,
Let my eyes see none but you!

O God, you are so magnificent! (give 3 times)
I AM, I AM, I AM adoring Thee! (give 9 times)
O God, you are so magnificent! (give 3 times)

My very own
Beloved I AM! Beloved I AM! Beloved I AM!

THE LIGHT OF GOD
NEVER FAILS!

Instructions:

This fiat is so easy to remember, you can use it in any situation. If you're stuck in traffic, about to go into a tough meeting or faced with an onslaught of negative energy from others, simply say it, silently or aloud, and watch as God's light moves into action.

The Light of God never fails!
The Light of God never fails!
The Light of God never fails!
and the Beloved Mighty I AM Presence
is that Light!

I AM THE ONENESS OF LIFE

Instructions:

Use this decree to feel loved, fulfilled and connected to God. As you give it, try to remember the feeling of your original oneness with God and know that you can have that feeling always—just by contacting your I AM Presence.

Visualization:

This is another decree that calls for a pink visualization. The pink represents God's love, which enfolds, comforts and protects all of us. See yourself surrounded by a soft rose-petal-pink light. Imagine that you are being drawn upward to the level of your I AM Presence. See yourself again becoming one with God.

I AM the Wholeness of the circle of infinity
I AM the fulfillment of the longing
    for Wholeness
I AM the return to the state of Oneness
    in God
I AM contemplation of the Oneness of Life
I AM entering the Oneness of Life
I AM experiencing the Oneness of Life
I AM the Oneness of Life
I AM in the center of a rose
I AM the flaming fire of that Oneness
I AM in the center of God's consciousness
I AM the bursting forth of the energies
   · of the heart inundating cosmos,
    filling all space, becoming part of all time
And thus I cannot remain separate, apart,
    alone
I AM the one Flame
I AM the one Flame of Life
    blazing upon the altar of being

I AM the Oneness of Life
I AM the Oneness of Life
I AM the Oneness of Life

NOTES

1. Dr. William Nolan, quoted in Larry Dossey, M.D., *Healing Words: The Power of Prayer and the Practice of Medicine* (HarperSanFrancisco, 1993), p. 180.

2. Statistics taken from a *Time*/CNN poll conducted in June 1996 by Yankelovich Partners.

3. See "Sound Waves May Drive Cosmic Structure," *Science News* 151, 11 January 1997.

4. Dr. Alfred A. Tomatis, quoted in Tim Wilson, "Chant: The Healing Power of Voice and Ear," in *Music: Physician for Times to Come,* ed. Don Campbell (Wheaton, Ill.: Theosophical Publishing House, Quest Books, 1991), p. 13.

5. Exod. 3:2. All Bible verses are from the King James Version unless otherwise noted.

6. The Ascended Masters teach that the Holy Christ Self (corresponding to God the Son)

is the Universal Christ individualized for each of us. The Holy Christ Self is your inner teacher, guardian, friend and advocate before God. The I AM Presence (corresponding to God the Father) is the absolute perfection of your divine reality. It is the Spirit of the living God individualized for each of us.

7. Exod. 3:15 (emphasis added).

8. John 11:25.

9. Sergius Bolshakoff, *Russian Mystics* (Kalamazoo, Mich.: Cistercian Publications, 1980), pp. 232, 233.

10. *A Discourse on Abba Philimon,* in *The Philokalia,* comp. St. Nikodimos of the Holy Mountain and St. Makarios of Corinth, trans. G. E. H. Palmer, Philip Sherrard, and Kallistos Ware, 3 vols. (London: Faber and Faber, 1981), 2:349.

11. Mal. 3:10.

PICTURE CREDITS

BOOKS AND CASSETTES ON
THE CREATIVE POWER OF SOUND

AUDIO

Decrees and Songs

HEALING MEDITATIONS
1 cassette   70 min.   #A94118 $7.50

LOVE MEDITATIONS
1 cassette   70 min.   #A95046 $7.50

DEVOTIONS, DECREES AND SPIRITED
SONGS TO ARCHANGEL MICHAEL
1 cassette   70 min.   #A93090 $8.95

SAVE THE WORLD WITH VIOLET FLAME!
TAPE 1
1 cassette   90 min.   #B88019 $7.50

FIATS! FIATS! FIATS!
1 cassette   66 min.   #B96060 $9.50
1 CD   67 min.   #D96060 $14.95

DECREES AND SONGS BY MARK L. PROPHET
2-cassette album   3 hr.   #A8202 $14.95

Lecture

THE SCIENCE OF THE SPOKEN WORD:
WHY AND HOW TO DECREE EFFECTIVELY
by Mark and Elizabeth Prophet
4-cassette album   6 hr.   #A7736 $29.95

BOOKS

THE SCIENCE OF THE SPOKEN WORD
by Mark L. Prophet and Elizabeth Clare Prophet
softbound   218 pages   #104 $11.95

PRAYER AND MEDITATION
by Jesus and Kuthumi
softbound   305 pages   #569 $10.95

HOW TO WORK WITH ANGELS
book   114 pages   4"x 6"   #4445 $4.95

ANGELS
(mantras, decrees, prayers and songs)
booklet   18 pages   #3600 $3.95

HEART, HEAD AND HAND DECREES
booklet   32 pages   4"x 5⅝"   #4444 $2.00

PRAYERS, MEDITATIONS AND DYNAMIC
DECREES
SECTION I: 104 decrees   #105 $4.95
SECTION II: 75 decrees   #1657 $4.95

To place an order, request our free catalog, or for information about seminars and conferences with Elizabeth Clare Prophet, write Summit University Press, Dept. 808, PO Box 5000, Corwin Springs, Montana 59030-5000 USA. Fax 1-800-221-8307 (406-848-9555 outside the U.S.A.) or E-mail us at tslinfo@tsl.org. Web site: http://www.tsl.org.

Elizabeth Clare Prophet is a pioneer of modern spirituality. She has written such classics of spiritual literature as *The Lost Years of Jesus*, *The Lost Teachings of Jesus*, *Saint Germain On Alchemy*, *Reincarnation: The Missing Link in Christianity*, *Kabbalah: Key to Your Inner Power* and *Quietly Comes the Buddha: Awakening Your Inner Buddha-Nature*.

Since the 1960s, Elizabeth Clare Prophet has been conducting conferences and workshops throughout the United States and the world on spiritual topics, including angels, the aura, soul mates, prophecy, spiritual psychology, reincarnation, the mystical paths of the world's religions and practical spirituality.

She has been featured on NBC's *Ancient Prophecies* and A&E's *The Unexplained* and has talked about her work on *Donahue, Larry King Live, Nightline, Sonya Live* and *CNN & Company*. She lives in Corwin Springs, Montana.

OTHER TITLES FROM

SUMMIT UNIVERSITY 🌀 PRESS®

Quietly Comes the Buddha:
Awakening Your Inner Buddha-Nature

Kabbalah: Key to Your Inner Power

Reincarnation:
The Missing Link in Christianity

The Lost Years of Jesus

The Lost Teachings of Jesus
BOOK 1 *Missing Texts • Karma and Reincarnation*
BOOK 2 *Mysteries of the Higher Self*
BOOK 3 *Keys to Self-Transcendence*
BOOK 4 *Finding the God Within*

The Human Aura

Saint Germain On Alchemy

Creative Abundance

How to Work with Angels

Access the Power of Your Higher Self

Violet Flame to Heal Body, Mind and Soul

Summit University Press titles are available
from fine bookstores everywhere, including
Barnes and Noble, B. Dalton Bookseller,
Borders, Hastings and Waldenbooks.